WHERE IS EVERYONE!

A Scientific Companion

WHERE IS EVERYONE!

Elizabeth
ZUBA

This book is dedicated to all the autonauts of every species and cosmic order, who need no reminder that any shadows or light that might move over these pages while reading should be considered illustrations, sometimes diagrams!

Printed in the United States of America

ISBN: 979-8-9883272-5-7

Published by Conduit Books & Ephemera
788 Osceola Avenue
Saint Paul, Minnesota 55105
www.conduit.org

Book design by Scott Bruno/b graphic design

Distributed by Itasca Books
www.itascabooks.com

Cover image: "The animal kingdom, illustrated!" circa 1872, Gibson & Co., Cincinnati, Ohio. Courtesy the Library of Congress.

CONTENTS

On Beginnings 1
The Dawn of Time 4
On the Stuff of Life 5
On Atoms and Disappearing 7
More On Atoms and Disappearing 9
How Things Grow 10
On Space and Time 12
On Shapes and Sizes 15
Why Things Grow Up 17
More on Why Things Grow Up 19
More on Space and Time 22
On Cycles and Returnings 23
On Knowing, Kind Of 25
On the Senses, Part I 28
More on Shapes and Sizes 31
Why We Are Here 32
On the Whole Animal, Vegetable, Mineral, Part I 33
On the Whole Animal, Vegetable, Mineral, Part II 35
Why Things Grow Old 37
On Gravity and Goings 38
On the Senses, Part II 40
More on What Bodies Know 43
On the Senses, Part III 44
On the Senses, Part IV 46
More on Knowing, Kind Of 47
On the Senses, Part V 50
On Systems and Stayings 52
More on Systems and Stayings 53
More on Why Things Grow Old 55
What Bodies Know 57
More on Cycles and Returnings 59
On Nature's Alphabet 60
On the Senses, Part VI 62

What Happens Next 63
On the Sun (Which Can Die but Not Energy) 65
On Insides and Outsides 66
On The Senses, Part VII 67
On Water and Habitats 69
On the Senses, Part VIII 71
On Forces and Motions 72
On Why Things Die 74
On Endings Generally 75

Notes 79
Acknowledgments 83
About the Author 85

Let it be softer than feathers!
Let the beginnings begin!
Where the sun is the other wing, come to take rest!

Where Is Everyone!

On Beginnings

Where an ostrich egg is just as big as a crocodile's! And the tiny minnow hails from a walloping blueberry! And the yawp of the meager egg is O my people O! And *it beats me* why we call a fish egg an egg and not a horse's or human's! Even though they're just the same of course, as anyone can plainly see, other than the whole inside-outside thing but who can ever tell insides from outsides anyway? Plus you could just as much say there's no white to eat like for the chicks, or anything to crack out of in the first place, more water womb into milk womb just like any other so-called mammal, but nobody ever does say that, they still just call a fish egg an egg! But I guess that's just the nature of these itsy-bitsy pictures my friends, glinting bright in the morning light on the whole idea of the whole life in one, I'm saying the whole idea of the whole life in the whole body in one, which is just like when someone dies and you can't remember them in any one particular way, you remember them in all their ages at once, *all their stages at once,* blue is the work of man, O now what roundness circles back at the tail?

*

I mean to go back to the little black speck of fish that may or may not become a full-grown fish depending on other circumstances that happen all the time and that's OK! Lest anyone think this is a treatise on life, because it is emphatically not, it is a treatise on death! Which is actually the whole point of eggs! Like how sometimes the river smells like honey but then other times like sulfur, depending on where you happen to be on the river, or whether or not anyone is even standing there watching the river at all in the first place, and this is one of the stories we tell ourselves that tell us where we come from. Ayekah.

*

Sing. Muse. Now I demand the meaning of sulfur. Now I demand the meaning of morning glory. A face grows from a boundary not a bloom.

The Dawn of Time

We imagine the world so badly. Who's to say there weren't any galactic birds, or at least something we might think of as birds, that sang out just before the Dawn of Time, just like any other dawn sings out right before it comes alive and so signaled the ever-present and simultaneous, parallel and inverted, accompaniment to accompaniment straight from the very beginning?! Which is definitely not something anyone can prove, or at least not yet anyway, and probably isn't even true! But it *is* singing. Which is just as important to remember. Where the sun is the other wing, come to take rest.

On the Stuff of Life

O isle, unto me! A leaf, a light! Light wind the swallows' sleep, really a kind of coasting! Listen, the only answer to Where do all the animals roam upon the earth, is that they do *not* roam upon the earth, that they have *never* roamed upon the earth, and that upon the earth there is only the sea and the air and the canopy of the body, which is all there ever was and all there ever will be! O now what sails out on the breath of man? Also why the further you go up on the food chain the more dead you are over the wires than alive in the first place, I mean really, take out all the dead in your blood and what are you left with? Air! That's it! So now if anyone ever asks you what human beings are made of, you've got the answer, and why biology classes don't start with the anatomy of death is a mystery to me, but probably has something to do with the soft break of the moving space of one body where it overlaps with the moving space of another, hope I guess in the soaring, for I have given you an example that you should do as I have done.

*

Or some might say existential dread a little too early in life, but it seems to me we'd all be a lot better off with the mystery of living all dead like this right from the very beginning, Nothing, I'm saying in a Dickinson way, under the shade of the gingko trees, following the call of the sirens down to the beaches of Brooklyn where the water pours out in thick gardens of simple-but-very-much-more-alive-than-human-beings jellyfish, where we should all be going right now, into the jellyfish folds! To nurse in their long gentle breaths of pink pink forever! I am the tooth of the ripened fruit, nay, the largest tooth. Come! It's time to gather ourselves within us or never be found.

On Atoms and Disappearing

Because there are no fiery stars fallen to earth, who hasn't held the tail of a shucked pea in their hands and fed it softly into their mouths? The whole bean life right there split down the middle, the leaves, the roots, the next leaves, the leaves after that, all tucked-in and arriving, little marched amplings of time in the middle, time unto time! Just like our very own hands themselves but only if our very own hands were actually holding everything they ever held before or after they ever held them and still looked just the same as our same old hands on account of everything being so shrunk down as to be effectively invisible in order to pack it all in so you can never really see the full picture, kind of like that super thin paper in giant texts that's actually called scritta paper but usually just called bible paper, in dictionaries and bibles of course, where you can see both sides of the page at once plus sometimes the under ones and the overtop ones too, one way of seeing more of everything all together, being so costly and unwieldy, even though you can't read the other side exactly, but you can still see it! O where are your hands in your hands now? Picking the harebells.

*

I guess you could call it a kind of everybody-talking-at-once! Even though some people say a word is just a sound you're making. An illustration of illustration, the way the air flees into the skin, and even the sky is planted with a three-centimeter-thick branch to land on that will eventually break and get carried off somewhere by whatever animal, vegetable, or mineral might come along and want to claim it. Pile it branch over branch. I you we blue.

More on Atoms and Disappearing

So that a bull doesn't see red at all but a chicken will devour its own wing, wet the cheeks of the living. I guess you can read these stories as stories or patterns for creation. My friends! Morning ripens onto our land.

How Things Grow

Plus now, today! Dancing is so much better than it used to be when it was just everybody in a circle, on account of all the unsuspecting people who come and go just as they please, and make any intentional steps appear even more incredible but also simultaneously even more invisible, which is really a very unwitting and refreshing kind of dancing! Kind of like how many infusoria you might be swallowing on any given night swimming in the Hudson and not ever knowing it! Not to mention whatever else you might be swallowing, even though most people don't even put their heads under anymore, which is probably a good thing, actually infusoria is just an obsolete term for protista, but obviously a much better one, and the point is they're big feelers too, feeling their way around toward any there or not there in clouds of everybody's-welcome-so-come-on-in! And apparently you can cultivate them yourself just by soaking the skin of a papaya in "aged" water, and your guess is as good as mine what aged water means but definitely the Hudson is aged so maybe something like the Hudson, not the perishable but the imperishable. The imperishable seed.

*

Plus infusoria even with no nervous system at all can still respond to environmental stimuli, I don't know if you could say *learn* exactly, but then learning isn't necessarily a full-body experience anyway. Take the anemone for example, a full 10,000 times bigger than your average infusoria and with its brain right there around its mouth to boot, learning all the difference you like between little bits of meat and little bits of blood-soaked blotting paper on the one tentacle and never telling any of the other tentacles anything at all about it, and could very well end up eating its own weight in paper before it realizes it's been tricked only to do it all over again the next day! People say I-Will-Be-What-I-Will-Be isn't really the best translation because biblical Hebrew didn't distinguish between tenses, but don't get excited because that means I-Am-Becoming-Who-I-Am-Becoming is also wrong.

On Space and Time

What is *The revolution of cells is upon us? The revolution of cells is upon us* is what should be added to the wall text of drawing exhibits everywhere, even if all you have is a pencil, and even though most pencils are made of cedar and cedars have tree rings whereas tropical trees have none on account of their constant spring growth, I guess you could say you can't have one without the other, winter and spring I mean! Which is actually just like fingerprints, or rather how fingerprints make themselves into fingerprints, the blooming and the burying, only the seasons don't have anything to do with it, that was just a metaphor! But metaphorically speaking it's definitely true that the top layer is a kind of springtime, for human skin I'm saying, and the bottom more of a tundra in terms of its slow-mo growth so that the top layer literally shoots right out over the bottom, collapsing down into the sides of its own winter, buckling into little mini-ridges and valleys, cold and stark across the field, and even now! They buckle. O tell me what seasons fall from our hands! Cover your roof in mud, and it will be covered in seeds.

*

But such is the nature of seeds! Even though it can be pretty hard to get enough pressure from a pencil the way you can with a pen, I mean in terms of welting deep into the wall so that it really takes a good amount of sanding to remove any residual inscription on the inner surface like if a drought came along one summer or insects one year ate up all the leaves, which almost never happens to century plants, and is yet another example of timeless vegetation that doesn't actually bloom every hundred years but more like every ten or twenty (maybe more depending on the climate) and so being less time-oriented and more space-oriented really gets to the whole point of how things are a returning, I'm saying like how Kenneth Patchen said it, not returning, but *a returning*.

✳

O the tips of my hands upon the tips of my hands. And a going, a going, and the stars.

On Shapes and Sizes

Just look at the trout and the tree! Where your fingers are ships unto the sea of heaven and the sea of heaven is bounded steeply by the sea of the earth! Not that they grow the same way exactly, trout having all their future trout parts straight from the very beginning, like all their future trout bones that actually do grow like trees, but that's on the inside, whereas on the *outside* a trout just looks like a little trout getting bigger and bigger into a bigger trout, but still the same trout, which is not at all like trees that grow right out of themselves, with their second and third limbs growing high above their first limbs and so forth and so on, right on up high unto the sea of heaven! I guess you could say trout are more like little wrapped Christo trees in the freshwaters of the earth but it's still nice to imagine baby trout growing straight up out of their heads anyway! Like the heads of our heads, even now, they dance upon the water!

*

Not that you can ever age trout, or trees for that matter, by their size exactly, since any number of earthly interventions might have come along and stunted or spurred their growth, like sea-stars, which are neither trout nor trees but more trees than trout actually, formally known as star-fish, whose five finger-branches may or may not ever grow at all depending on what they have to eat, so that just a few months after birth one sea-star might be several-thousand times bigger than its twin sibling sea-star, still bobbing along the size of the head of a pin somewhere on account of being swept away by whatever wave happened to come along and rob it of the chance to dine on a few barnacles before getting caught up in the forces of habitat, and the point is! Any sea-star in your hand might be nothing but a baby star or a very old grandma star and you can never know the difference, but even if you *could* know the difference, you'd still have to keep your eye on the number of branches! OK, here's a riddle. If five trees braid themselves up like the sea into the wind, what grows by the gaze of their branching? What, I ask you, breaches the arc?

Why Things Grow Up

Staircases are the practice of angels. Beneath the blade, weeps the fruit. Beneath the dragon, beats the hundred hearts of dragons. I'm thinking about the spiral ones that spin up high into retreating eyeballs, like the natural progression from gun powder to kaboom, mass to speed, like those fireworks that corkscrew their way up high into the sky and have that feeling of extra speedy speed despite obviously being slower than linear fireworks, which you know for a fact in your brain but something about the spiral makes them more of a *how* than a *what* just the same, like how Louise Bourgeois's hair paintings spiral all the way down into her lungs and then back out and around the sun and out and out and on forever, you have to imagine! Which I guess makes Fibonacci both right and not right in terms of the divinity part, and when did we stop saying forty-leven anyway? O now what carries the one? I don't know, but it definitely has something to do with the short-end of things keeping up the long-end, which is one of the things the duchess tells Alice.

✳

Also, take care of the sense, and the sounds will take care of themselves! And verily I tell you, the best way to find out the best way to go up or down any particular spiral staircase is just to see how well the people before you did it, and whether or not they slipped or tripped or fell back down, and then just copy whatever they did or didn't do, because when it comes right down to it the sound of pounding feet over any vertical distance is almost always just as enchanting, dare I say hopeful, as the movement itself, and no matter how many spirals there are in the fanned-out dress around a dancer's body, you can still stomp around it in a circle and imagine the rumble of your feet like for a gathering turn.

More on Why Things Grow Up

Plus all sun-bleached things are a kind of nebulae if you look at them close enough, like how garlic pollen-grains look like flying saucers and evening primrose just like Saturn, look! O barriers of the cosmos! Which is also why different ancient peoples used to go out every year and cut down wild date palm branches along the riverbanks, just to bring back and parade around their own date palm orchards, dancing and singing harvest songs like "Oats, Peas, Beans and Barley Grow" only a different version of course with more appropriate grains and fruits to their time and place, and you can probably just make up the jig part, but the moral of the story is, galactic pollen wilding the earth! You just can't have one without the other! Because calling the night sky a light show is almost always ridiculous unless you've ever been to one of those choral concerts where the singers all pour in from the back of the theater and then down the aisles and then climb up onto the stage in waves, which makes you feel like you're waving too and is probably the point.

*

Some non-Freudian psychologists say the whole reason we say *falling* in and out of love is on account of our own human orientation of limited space, but Michaux talks about accidentally walking on the ceiling instead of the ground in a moment of distraction, so I'm not sure how that plays into *love* per se but it works for space and bodies, like how one little yellow pollen-grain on a single strand of silk makes for one little yellow kernel in an otherwise solid white ear of corn, so really you have to ask yourself! Where are you falling now?

✳

And what about the seeds of potatoes that practically no one uses to grow anything anymore? I mean against all reason, the barrel-shaped pollen-grains of potatoes burying their faces into the bleached, bleached hands of the earth?

More on Space and Time

Two fingerprints diverged in a wood. Good thing they were tied together! Actually it's common practice all over the world to give camels the hides of their dead calves to let down their milk, also cows. Which is just proof again that holding is only *ever* a remembering. All along the palms of your hands, even now you can touch them. There. A leathering of the light.

On Cycles and Returnings

Some people say chicken-of-the-woods is called chicken-of-the-woods on account of the way it sticks out from the tree just like how chickens stretch out their necks and pop up onto the tips of their toes at the first sign of any kind of atmospheric circus come up off the trees, in long silent tails that string out from your hands and momentarily bathe you in some kind of backwards time just before you realize you better get shaking, I mean weathervanes don't look like chickens for nothing, people! But then other people say no, it's on account of the color and feather-like cascades down the side of the tree and then even *other* people say it's because of the texture, but obviously those people are talking about cooked chicken, and into the wind the body of the bloom. But really, just think how no matter which way you turn an egg around the yolk always goes right back up to the top, chicken eggs but probably true for all eggs, right back up like a barrel at sea or a barrel at river or even a barrel at little creek in the earth because obviously it doesn't actually end anywhere! The sea I mean, not the barrel.

*

And even as I say this I'm at sea which is also the clouds, but that's another cycle! And *still* has everything to do with the way the air washes through all the little invisible holes of an eggshell, I mean for the oxygen, to get back to the chicken, I'm saying once the yoke-umbilical-cord dries up and it starts to get the idea that it's time to crack out of there. Listen! We better prepare our teeth around us to take us with us at last.

On Knowing, Kind Of

And while we're at it, it's totally natural to read "starlathered" as "slaughtered," so don't ever feel bad if that happens to you, I mean first of all they have practically all the same letters, not to mention shared root words, and that's even before you get to the over-cuppeth of running, and who can ever expect to read "starlathered" anyway? Like that parrot who only knew how to say, "My feathers are not a tail because I cannot wag them," and who could ever expect a parrot to say that? Every creature on earth denying their own existence, actually any bird can be taught to sing the song of any other bird if you isolate it and play a recording of the other bird's song on repeat, which people used to have to pay for and pretty steeply too, but now it's free on youtube! So that the second bird learns the first bird's song so well it replaces its own song entirely, and then that way when the first bird dies, its song will live on safe and sound in the second bird, although also meaning that now the second bird's song is lost forever, which is maybe OK on an occasional basis but the problem is when it's happening across whole species, and genetically and generationally all the way down to the very last bird on earth. (The only one, muttered the bird.) I mean obviously, but it happens.

✳

Which makes me think of Kafka's Josephine who died by her own piping, so to speak, strike a bell and touch your fingernail to its edge for just as long as you can feel the bell moving. And wait for the others to join us. Actually, one way of explaining to children how different languages developed is to say One day the children traveled too far from home and being all alone and with no adults to teach them, had to start all over. Which happens, which happens.

*

Wrest Identity from Nothing shouldn't be said for anything but how Baldwin meant it and yet it falls everywhere upon the mouths of the earth, upon the mouths of our mouths, like the margins of fruit, like the margins of margins.

On the Senses, Part I

The time has come to talk about the senses, a highly under-developed area of science! And what better place to start than the eyeballs, fashioned more for touching than seeing, and mostly for turning you around no matter what you learned in school, and even though it feels like you're the one turning them, but that's just part of the upside-down perception of sight, which you probably already know about, and is also totally easily proven! All you have to do is cover your right eye,—you can do it now if you want to—and try following the direction of the wind with your left eye, but not if it's not a particularly windy day because it can be hard to feel the wind with just one eyeball so a little extra wind can help, and just watch how you start loping around on your left leg like a maypole! Which has absolutely nothing to do with the wind being circular at all, because it isn't, and even though your eyeball is, spherical I mean, but that's also completely irrelevant, and is actually not at all true for most other animals, I'm saying that they'd spin around like a one-eyed maypole, despite having spherical eyeballs just the same, on account of their brains *already* being perfectly balanced hemispherically-speaking and thus in no need to be righted back into position whatsoever!

✳

O for what have I come if not to find you? And really it all comes down to something people used to call the thinking side or the language side, even though now we know it's a little less simple than that, just in case you wanted to try covering one of the eyes of your favorite domesticated beast and giving it a whirl, unless your favorite domesticated beast is a monkey of course! And really it makes for a lovely picture if you happen to try it on a beach or a maybe a gravel driveway, I'm saying if you're a human or a monkey, and left to your own circular symptoms of force and time, the ring patterns left in the sand, or in the sky for that matter, which is also why it's actually not at all unusual to become ambidextrous if you lose your dominant eye, on account of the hand-eye connection, i.e. the brain-eye connection, and so being one-eyed you would immediately stop loping in any one direction, no matter which eye you covered, which could just as well have been your left eye, I didn't mean to exclude the lefties! So if that's you, just read this all over again but with the other eye.

*

And this, my friends, is why the people of the earth pray not to be heard but to see. Amen.

More on Shapes and Sizes

Where the light turns the tree and the little dam gives way to vertical running. What wipes the milk from the body? The blood from the living? Harebells upon harebells quick along the leaf. I guess you could call it a kind of putting-together, a carrying-over tenderly, tenderly. Like how the little brown ants recognize their fellow little brown ants by holding them, but not just by holding them, stretching their whole bodies out one onto the other. Do you know me, Bert?

Why We Are Here

To the thumb, inaudible! To the ear, the unseen eyes of a honey bee! O now what holds the golden bricks of early morning lighting up the grass? Maybe somebody told Brancusi a glorious death was less noble than a struggle and that's why you almost never find hands on his sculptures, only pretend hands, but not the kind where you can actually count out any individual fingers, the only one I can think of is The Kiss. I've heard some people say if you don't sit at the piano every day you'll never grow all eight of your fingers and two thumbs, not to their fullest lengths anyway, and it isn't so much that we *know* otherwise, but that we *choose* otherwise, strangely filled with the breath of the sky. Once, a starling, all alone came in! The thing is even if you were to get hit in the head right now, I mean sure it might be in the bells and whistles spot, but it might just as well be in the singing spot or even the little Beethoven igniting the nerve-strumming pyre sunspot spot! So who's to say what you might yet carry or not carry with you?! Listen, everyone will tell you if you want to learn to be a sculptor with a block of stone in your hands, you have to start by looking for the memory of the stone, but that's 100% bullshit. You have to put down that stone and sit in your hands.

On the Whole Animal, Vegetable, Mineral, Part I

Green is the color of electricity asleep and soon the sun will come out and run around! The truth is you can never say exactly what plants know or don't know, but you *can* say they make good decisions, or usually do anyway, and some people say that's just as good as knowing, maybe even better! Not that I'm saying that but you can see the reason behind it, like if a deer or a strong wind were to come along and lop off the top bit of a baby pine trunk, the baby pine would just reroute one of its branches and abracadabra new trunk! Of course it can happen that it might make a mistake and end up with two trunks, maybe even three, but it's rare and everybody makes mistakes sometimes, especially babies, and frankly babydom can be a *very* long time depending on the species, like how Whitman used to say he could only write what life told him to, and that's saying something! I mean just think how runner plants grow away from the sun against all natural instinct, but really that's just because the ground is the only thing that they can stay hanging onto and so in the long run, O run, their leaves and flowers do indeed grow back toward the light, and that's just part of the pre-package package of runner plants. Also other animals.

✳

Where blindness breaks quick along the blade of the body. Go ahead, I dare you, try explaining to a judge that the very question of separating emotion from reason is just about the dumbest thing you've ever heard, and no, you definitely *cannot* swear that your emotions wouldn't "count" in any decision you make, plus only insane people or sleeping people think their own distorted versions of reality are actually true without a second thought as to what the sun or trees or anybody else is thinking! I mean who isn't waiting for something they can't see? OK, now we will sit here and watch the green green filaments flee from the earth.

On the Whole Animal, Vegetable, Mineral, Part II

But then other people say plants are really just sluggish animals, not as sluggish as water clams but close! Which is exactly the same thing that Nietzsche said about human beings being human beings on account of their capacity to promise, and I don't see how anyone could argue otherwise, I mean about plants being animals at least. Eo ipso! My people! If the sweeping radial tip of any climbing plant—hops and honeysuckle left, bean and morning glory right—isn't the word before the deed, I don't know what is, so maybe a better definition would be something like, Any more than the sun stretches across the afternoon, nestles long into the hand, doubt thou the stars are fire.

✳

Then again it's just as true that any leaf or tendril will turn toward any red hot wire if it's bright enough and warm enough, inching slowly toward the light until it burns itself to death, which I did try at home once and very much wish I hadn't, but even that still holds really, I mean in terms of plants being animals! But then other people say no, plants aren't animals at all, not in any way whatsoever on account of everything vegetable actually just being a way to make the sun directly visible, so you and every other animal can just stare and stare into the sun at no risk of retinal damage whatsoever, like a sun-mirror but without the cancer, which is also why it has to go both ways around, to get back to the climbing plants, I'm saying the one way for the sun and the other for the earth, so there goes that theory, and even the harebells, look! They bend to bury their dead.

Why Things Grow Old

Spirals like seafoam ripening. Am I a falcon, or a storm, or a song? Is Rilke who didn't even know the spark of life is an actual real thing, I mean when the sperm enters the egg and the calcium gives way to zinc and the zinc explodes in a zap of white light where it wrestles the extracellular space to the ground. Limps out into the morning. Funnels the arc.

On Gravity and Goings

The fact is any tree, given half a chance and a good set of wings, would shoot up into the sky just the same as any other heliotropic animal mouth open in ecstatic rapture, coming home at last, I mean why wouldn't it?! What's the difference between a tree and a moth anyway? I'm saying in terms of pyrolatry, even in caterpillar form they go streaming up into the sun, up up up to the very end of that spring branch that—O look—just happens to have a new leaf! Though admittedly it's too bad they can't seem to hold onto more of that stop-at-the-leaf instinct once they have wings and not fling themselves heedlessly into light bulbs, but then again, maybe that's the whole point, outgrow the stop-at-the-leaf instinct to finally get there, to get to the light! Because, let's be honest, there are lights you can get to and lights you can't get to, regardless of what flies unbonneted through the gates, but tell that to the raining caterpillars, not to mention that that tree was probably living there just fine for some two hundred odd years before suddenly being ravaged to death, on account of all those damn larvae, but maybe that's another story, plus Ponge already proposed replacing the lyrical O! with the infinity symbol ∞! ages ago, and if we hadn't learned by then to let significance work itself out on its own, my friends, we probably never would.

✳

Not that any pilgrimage, regardless of size or purpose, wouldn't be just as meaningful without the right number of steps, but just that any breath is almost always conic no matter what kind of mouth it's coming out of, caterpillar or otherwise, a little like rocket exhaust, so I'm not sure what the ∞ even does for a song in the first place! Because when we break bitterly against the light, we break bitterly against the light and fall to the earth by the heat of our mouths.

On the Senses, Part II

Sometimes after any kind of -ectomy you can't remember things, which is not at all related to whatever it is you're missing now, probably self-evident by whatever you were -ectomying, but rather on account of the *way* you're missing it, like how sorrows and seasons ripen fields and reposing hours. Nowhere near the fields, and yet still they ripen! And really it's so easy to lump all the inside-inside senses into one sixth sense, even though there's actually more like twenty or thirty, maybe more, depending on how you carve up the brain or perceive your body in space, which of course is totally different from any other person's body in space, like how any one person's upness is a totally different sensation from any other person's upness, just as one little example of pretty much everything when it comes to orientation and perception on account of all the things that make an outside environment inside, or an inside outside, just ask the jellyfish! Or water! But then I have no idea how these things might apply to other animal brains, so I'll just stick to people. Dear people, the substance of sense follows the substance of shadow, no matter what you do.

✳

I mean what kid doesn't know that after you whirl yourself around in one direction until you're totally dizzy and can hardly stand up, you just have to whirl yourself back around in the other direction to get your brain back into its first place in the first place. Before not before I am, I am again, all ye little children, crawl back in time into the cradle of arms that remember you.

*

But *even then* sometimes you'll still forget and stay too long after everything is over, which I had no intention of doing the other night, but then somebody said, That's OK, that's the whole idea of these kinds of parties anyway, I mean how nothing is staying and staying is going and what is going has always stayed, both exiled and returned, O tonight so blindly it turns.

More on What Bodies Know

Some diagrams you have to imagine. A pair of cows hauls a milk wagon up the hill. The sun breaches what it doesn't submerge. Nerves grow right off their own tips like branches, bit by fractal bit right off the ends, bridging their own bridges to get wherever they're going, bending their gentle knees into the light. Can you see them? O my friends, some configurations answer only the flying kinds of questions, the very questions you've been waiting for since the day you were born! Like how *do* they wake in the morning? The cows, I mean. What's the first thing they see? And do they hear the others breathing?

On the Senses, Part III

So just remember, anyone who claims they know all the senses is whistling out their back teeth and what they're whistling is Dixie! Now we will strap transistor radios to our waists. Now we will make fish for people. Just take for one little example O Groping Hands, obviously never officially named or it would have a much more reductive name to go by, but anyway the one everybody just calls O Groping Hands! Generally described as the feeling of things in your hands that aren't there at all but somewhere else entirely because your hands have suddenly traveled far away from themselves like when you're fishing and you feel a pull on the line and you think you're feeling the line in your hands where you can see them but really your hands are all the way down at the end of the line where the fish is pulling, and now where also your hands are pulling, even though ostensibly your hands are right in front of you and not even touching the line at all! Not that I personally know anything about fishing, but the point is you can never predict which way your body might be coming from, or for that matter where it might suddenly be going! Hasten quick your touch to its certain end.

✳

And really who could ever predict that one would start playing Moon River on the way home? I mean the radios, not the fish, which was wild! And made me think of the field as a river and the trees as fish and how we never say the pear trees in the field are pulling hard on the light, hooked and desperate in the grass, but why don't we say that? Come on, that could be exactly what the pear trees are doing, only we have no idea on account of them being in our tree-feeling blind-spot since we never go up to them and touch them, never actually feel them yanking at the other end, which is clearly something we should all be doing all the time! And is actually the whole reason for moons in rivers in the first place, I mean to be tied to what ties us. To be given death in human terms.

On the Senses, Part IV

Maybe time is like how some people hold balloons down with their chins when they have no hands. What is touch? Touch is the black shawl you lay over your head slowly. Makes the shape of death where it lands.

More on Knowing, Kind Of

Call it the thrill of the disappearing disappearing! A critical concept for any basic understanding of physics, also chemistry, which are really the same thing and we just divide them up on account of how we look at them, like those parlor games where I say chicken and you say whatever first pops into your head when I say chicken, or I could say vase and then you'd tell me whatever you saw in your head right at the exact moment I said vase, flowers or no flowers, clouds puddling the earth over the rim, but then somebody else entirely might say Birds of Paradise crowding the light with enchanted spritely prancing! In other words the kinds of games where you could either stop at flowers or no flowers, or go on and on until you're down to every last yes-or-no particulate, what some people call eye-mindedness, or It-From-Bit reality, which is what John Wheeler called it anyway, sight hidden from sight! All measurements limited to things that measure measurements! Regardless of the number of color cones in your eyes. But then there are other people who never see a *thing* at all, just letters. I mean when I say vase, all they see in their heads is the *word* vase, not any kind of actual thing, literal blossoms blown back onto the tree. Mapping the incompleteness of blossoms.

✳

Actually, contrary to what the tech-flesh-eaters say, lots of chess players play blind-folded all the time, on account of not-seeing having already been the best way to keep up any good old-fashioned seeing since *the dawn of time,* I mean in order to keep up all those scores of possible boards in their minds at any one time instead of being overpowered by their own eyeballs, so maybe that's the best way to look and then turn away and never see what's on your eyes at all? Like the ruby words beset the songs of the wood pigeons, maybe we should all just start wearing blindfolds now?

*

O when will we hear them whispering into the earth?

On the Senses, Part V

Now we will stand in a hole and blink the black, black ground. Now we will stand in a hole and scrape the ground from our tongues. What does the eye feel anyway? Sandpaper. Daffodil. Stone. I mean when you're looking at sandpaper, daffodils, stone! But that's when they're open, and then other times they have to be closed to feel what they need to be feeling, just like they need to be closed to see what they need to be seeing as was already demonstrated with the example of the chess players, so it's the same thing all over again, only with feeling this time! Take for example when people faint, I mean actually fall over and faint, they never see anything at all, which has nothing to do with suddenly being tired or anything of the sort, but rather because that way, eyes closed, internally north, they can only fall into themselves and not away from themselves, and this is the Law of the Body Falling Toward Center, which is one of those absolute laws that everybody lives by but just never even knows about! And truly if not for these kinds of automatic properties, people would be falling away from themselves left and right, and then where, I ask you, would we be?!

*

Not that there isn't a time for falling away from yourself, but just that it can be hard sometimes to find your way back again. O my friends, even now, you're nowhere to be seen. Like when Helen Keller wanted to know what jumping was and so held onto Merce Cunningham's gentle waist and bounced along. There's a video, you can find it. *So light,* she says, *like the mind.*

On Systems and Stayings

O the rain is falling! First it was the fish that put airholes all over their bodies, then the leaves, then the insects! Why didn't we? Kingdom upon kingdom? Breath upon breath? Oh well, I guess we have a couple. Under the sky, the rain shifts about your fingers, clutches your hands to its rising chest.

More on Systems and Stayings

What is instinct? Another word for body. All the leaves that open in the rain. Some people say human beings like to swim on account of some carry-over instinct from five hundred plus million years ago when we were confined to water, I mean when we were fish confined to being fish, surfing our hidden course upon the scale, and so that's why we like to swim and other animals, say the gorilla for example, have absolutely no interest in swimming whatsoever, which is obviously a very stupid thing to say, for all the evident reasons, and I wouldn't even mention it! Except I was just thinking that *then again* maybe there really is something to the way sometimes a drowning person just throws up their arms and surrenders, not even trying to beat back the engulfing water at all, but just raises their arms up over their head and sinks, which must be some kind of wayward instinct to climb up or climb out or climb off, on account of how we once escaped death by running up high into the trees, all our instincts concentrated by the gulf of falling that precedes us, bleeding quick on the heels of our own going.

*

Fasten Nothing to Nothing! Which I guess isn't so different from how people used to think different bird eggs had different shapes on account of different protective needs depending on their nests, like a grass nest or a tree nest or something like that, but then it turns out it has nothing to do with the egg or its so-called nest needs whatsoever! And really it's just the flight of the mother's body, I mean literally 3D-sketched by the flight of the mother's body, tender record, which of course is totally different bird to bird, but then there are so many arms that shape us, and the real question is, who among us will know the body of the tree when the time comes to climb the tree? And the answer is the gorilla. Only the gorilla will ever, *ever* know the body.

More on Why Things Grow Old

All things that are are trembling. Fluent of fires flowering. Flowering fires of atomic fluid-ing. Can you hear me now? Listen! All over the narrowing coasts of the Northeast of the U. S. of A., people still collect the ear stones of cod fish on account of their being lucky, although not as many as they used to since we pretty much killed off all the cod some fifty-odd years ago, though by all appearances they're making a come-back, which must mean they're even luckier now than they were before, or we can only hope! Also pretty much every animal has ear stones so I'm not exactly sure why cod fish ones are special in particular, but who can ever account for these kinds of believings? Where the earth trembled the earth, shook the foundations of the hills! And still we stand! Mostly anyway, even though it's really the ear drum that does all the actual hearing, but you can't deny they're both shaking baby, which should definitely make us all rethink quaking now.

*

Like how people hear almost everything better between their teeth if you bang at the other end with a fork or a stick, which is also related to several early American religions, and might even be the origin of ear stone-collecting, but that's pure conjecture mind you! And so, my sisters and brothers, the next time you're stuck in a crappy house in a storm, you just saddle up and listen to the window of the music of the spheres, O let him step to the music he hears however measured or far away! Which is what Thoreau had to say about breaking. Onto your very ground. Or would it be into? Into your very ground? Yes, it would.

What Bodies Know

Calling all trilogyisms! Delight for the delightful. Despair for the despairing. Trust for all that must be trusted now. Just think of the wearing of any skin thin and broken until eventually the rubbing only makes the cells work harder, so the skin folds in and the under-living pushes up its crown which now no work can wear through, and you can think of this as your hands, also shells! Earth upon the hand upon the sky! Blesséd are the triangles that hum into the night, even though almost no one ever really sees them in their entirety, on account of being in the dark half the time, so to speak, call it the under-under, just like the drone ants who are really more gentlemen of leisure or gentlemen of captivity depending on how you look at it and not at all like worker ants, who come and go just as they please, but then also do all the work, so it's a trade-off! But the point is, sometimes the drone ants, having little else to do, will take a morning stroll and wander down this path or the other, just to suddenly turn back around just as quick as they can on account of having gotten too close to the light and so shuffle their way back into the dark, except for when it's time to finally spread their wings and come out and die a little.

✳

Which is one of so many things that are good to think about when you're standing in front of the sea listening to the sea, like how some musicians tie gourds to their harps and Bacon smeared everything with his fist right at the end to make it human, or alive anyway, my friends! We usually think of heliotropism as turning toward the light but not true, not true! It just means *by* the light, turning *by* the light. And the skylarks fly high while they sing! And then they swoop down and sing too!

More on Cycles and Returnings

Transits of Venus. We dream the night sky in all the wrong pictures, flowers will never grow to love you. May be the purest sense of what we are doing on earth to no end of other directions, the way they drop their heads so close to the ground.

On Nature's Alphabet

What is the chemical symbol for oxygen? O my people O! Strung tight upon the body! A common anecdote but it bears repeating, by all accounts you can swim in a whole sea of snake venom, just as happy as any other beachgoer anywhere else on the planet just as long as you don't have any open wounds or put your head under, which is just as true as the one about poisonous snakebites being just a headache for pigs and not at all a death sentence like they are for humans on account of having no real bacon layer to give the blood half a fighting chance to catch up, like how the doors of a room open and close and now you know where the room is the breathiest, which is not at all bad information to have really, especially if you live with snakes, but the truth is the Big O just cycles wherever it wants to anyway, no matter how many open wounds you might have had or not had in the hypothetical venom ocean in the first place. Dead or alive makes no difference to the cosmo-sleep!

✳

Which is actually the whole reason the atomic number for oxygen is 8 to begin with, I mean because when somebody puts their head in the oven, even though there's plenty of oxygen in the blood, it's locked in so tight it can't get to the cells and so just circulates in the dark anyway, just the same as any other infinity symbol, trapped in its own cycling, which is obviously true for the O too, to get back to why oxygen is oxygen and not ixygen or some other vowel permutation of any sort, in and out just the same dead or alive, unbroken in its own planetary turn. Not that any of this really explains why Robert Seydel's balloon-heads don't just wipe away their heads, but somehow their entire bodies, because verily I tell you, you can cover those balloon-heads with your fist or your cheek or your mouth or anything at all, but no matter what you do, they will wipe away the body.

On the Senses, Part VI

What comes in dancing? *Sleck* and *linhorn*! Two colors I almost never saw! Not that I didn't make those names up, of course I did! But it's also totally possible I was gazing at *sleck* all morning and have been my whole life and just never knew it until that very moment I thought *sleck*, on account of previously assuming it was just a variation of the colors on either side of it, but such is the way of everything coming and going on earth, just ask the peepers! Like those dance numbers where the dancers run around together huddled in groups swerving left then right, circling back then forward, in a sort of flock, but not in-step, never in-step, which is so comforting, also heart-breaking because it's so human human to be out-of-step but also together, and, generally speaking, in-stepness is terrifying and who even likes those corps-de-ballet numbers, anyway? Because seeing is running and through which we must course our entire lives! Look, if you ever get a fresh cow eye from a farm up in Dutchess County and keep it all wrapped up in the dark for a few hours and then quick expose it to the light, you can process it just like any other roll of film in a bathroom and get your picture on a cow eyeball if you want to. It's true, we did it once with the kids. Speak, eyeball! How did you find me? What's my name?

What Happens Next

Probably rolling things, just think of the clouds and how they move their dark wave over the earth, so slow and steady you can almost predict the exact time you'll be able to lift your head back up and see the sun again, kind of like a giant stadium wave, only more head-bangy than arm-wavy, inverted and parallel or maybe symmetrical is the better word on account of the arc of the earth, you and everybody else ever before you and after you, lifting and lowering your head in time with the cloud-wave sweeping over the planetary curve, sweeping you onto the hour, Howdy Doody! My friend who's going blind says people don't use those tapping sticks anymore and the new ones have little balls at the end, even though the wheel was invented long before disease, and apparently everybody knows that, like how people washed their hands of responsibilities long before they even knew what bacteria was, innocent of this blood, plus there are biochemists working on bio-lighting *as we speak* to replace the energy-efficient lighting that replaced the incandescent lighting, harnessing the bioluminescence of fireflies or fish or bacteria, genetically engineering vines and birds to light up street lamps and windows, not that it would be hard for some enemy to take out that kind of an electrical system but it's not like it's hard now anyway! Also it would just grow back all over again, and who knows? Maybe they'll even genetically light up our eyeballs someday, not that that's the problem, but it would still be awesome.

*

But then I guess the thing about birds and fish and even vines for that matter, is how they exhaust every movement with their whole body, I mean how their whole body is really the wind, if you think about it. Tyger, Tyger, what moves my hands?

On the Sun (Which Can Die but Not Energy)

Because what we tell is a sort of prison anyway, like the hymn for the tail of a tadpole, a prayer, a circle, nothing, nowhere, so rarely enough. A kind of parallel search for the *where* of the body at the *when* of the body, O every morning the house flies measure their ears with their wings. And their ears are full of cardinals.

On Insides and Outsides

OK, here's a little practical advice. If you should ever get stuck with a needle from a barrel cactus, just rub the wound with some of its yellow waxy petals and that should clear it right up! Because once you start seeing this kind of orbiting around you, you'll start seeing it everywhere, just think of *surfaced* and *harnessed*, first the tooth, then the tongue.

On the Senses, Part VII

My fellow treegoers, where is everyone! I'm saying as an exclamation! The very reason interrogative words even became interrogative words in the first place, the weight of too much unknown, light upon the acid pail, soldering the stars! A matter of emphasis really, like how dogs don't *actually* smell any better than humans beings, or at least not *possibly* anyway, evolutionarily speaking, it's just that human beings tend to lean on sight and hearing more than taste and smell on account of L-A-N-G-U-A-G-E, I mean because we can see words and we can hear words but we can't taste them or smell them, or at least most people can't generally, whereas dogs, on account of not using words at all or at least not supposedly, think more in the smells and tastes range, which I guess means feeding your dog the same kibbles every day is a particularly cruel form of torture, and I'll have to start cooking for Lobster now! And even this, my friends, is a sowing!

*

Because any old man with an exceptionally long beard riding his bike along a back road can tell you how to make a bonsai by planting a seedling in an orange peel and trimming the roots as they poke through, but that's the easy part, the hard part is getting them to see the sun all gnarled and twisted on account of being gnarled and twisted makes for bad lumber so that's what stays behind to be remembered as a tree, I mean to be remembered as *a real tree*. Which is just to say, we carry goodbyes around our whole lives.

On Water and Habitats

Oceans are flowers. I am made fertile in the land of my affliction. Any terrestrial salamander halfway through being an egg will swim away and be aquatic forever if you crack it open and drop it in water, or at least that's how it was the last time I tried it! And really I have no idea if it works with other land animals with gills halfway through their egg-processes, I mean if you wanted to try branching out from salamanders, plus I'm not saying they'll all live happily ever after either, only that they'll live at all, although really there's no guarantee of that aquatically, terrestrially, or any other way about it, because the wind blows where it wishes and you can hear the sound of it! And truly if not for the egg-trapped salamanders, how *would* we move the spangled light across the water? Actually, lots of people think hatching living things and naming them are mutually exclusive and as soon as you do the one you've killed all possibility of the other, which doesn't really explain why so-called "worthless" stones in Japanese landscape art are just as important as "worthy" ones, clearly changing the whole meaning of *worthless*, as a name anyway, but it's still good to hope it might work with other things too, like the witness of a hand to the shape of whatever it's holding onto, or if the ocean had always been fresh water instead of saltwater, so too would our blood be fresh.

✳

Even though we'd still just call it blood! And never even know any different, owing to the *always* obviously, but then there are other stones in other parts of the world altogether where people write "I am but dust and ashes" on the one side of the stone and then, "For my sake, for my sake, the universe was created" on the other, and really it just depends on which side you happen to be on when you come along I guess.

On the Senses, Part VIII

On the subject of ashes, when Chang Bunker died in 1874, his brother Eng died two hours later on account of their shared circulatory system, even though the initial diagnosis from the autopsy was that he died of fright. Just ask anyone. Another way of seeing is by feeling the shake of whatever you're standing on.

On Forces and Motions

My friends, I wish you we! No dancing in Webster's visual dictionary but you can find Dalmania and Daman and Dandie Dinmont in that order, which I guess makes sense from a noun-verb perspective, I mean orienting visuals by things and not actions in action, which would obviously be a very tricky dictionary to write! Just like how some choreographers tell their dancers *what* to do or feel or think, but then others ask them *how* they do or feel or think in order to answer the first question in the first place, I'm saying the *what* question. For example, *What do you do to flee your own body?* starts with a *what* but is really a *how* question. What do you break to temper the dying? What flight of legs is always a thing falling? Which doesn't totally explain why horses run around on the tops of their middle fingers, in some kind of desperate raking of the earth, sky, earth, sky, earth! And might actually be a better explanation for the *Fuck you* finger being the *Fuck you* finger, not likely but it's a theory, I mean enacting actions in action, the rest of the hand abandoning its own desperation and clamoring back into the bone, which is more of a *what* to do or feel or think than a *how* anyway, so that's the moral of that story, *What do you do to rake against the sky?*

*

But then I guess all the fastest animals run around on their toes, not that you should put a ballerina in a 500 meter race, but even for a ballerina the whole hand on the ground or foot on the ground is strictly for stopping or sleeping or falling or dying, I'm saying to get back to the dying, loss into the palm, earth into the whole, and everything everything collapsing and flying. Which still doesn't explain why all the even-toed animals have horns at the sides of their heads and the odd-toed ones have none, but I mean not everything has a *reason*, galloping long into the cup of light, tell me now what bone hath reaped the body?

On Why Things Die

The way children know what to do with trees to find their faces, and the trumpet flowers suck in the blue and even your feet are little mountains, and the most human human movement is leaping but not the one done by the dancers who make a mockery of desperation. Agape. Agape. Because you run so sweetly.

On Endings Generally

Where we sing with our circular faces and descend from the bluebells! And even now some fleck of protoplasm is forging a whole new animal, and the wind is whistling and blows like a choir! Some people say it's the very hollowness of Medieval choral music that makes it sound so alive and so that's why it feels so sacred no matter what you believe or don't believe about the actual words, and Richard Powers says it's because it reminds us of how short a time we have a body, I guess he means all the wind, but anyway people tend to fall into two camps about it, the a-capellas-in-the-big empty chamber people and the monophonics. Personally, I'm with the monophonics because glee clubs don't do anything for me not even in a bathtub! Plus the single solitary melody sung in unison is the oldest being-alive feeling on earth, just ask the jellyfish, not to dismiss the minor minors, the minor minors are everything! But just that minorness is already part of anything done in unison anyway, as anyone who hides in the earth already knows and cannot ever stop from knowing, I'm saying the tree and the potter's field.

*

Not that any music would be much comfort to the mastodons now! To get back to the unison and the oldest being-alive feeling on earth, like the ones they found in Siberia a few years ago after the sled dogs ate them for dinner, which I guess must mean the mastodons are the new sled dogs, and the new sled dogs are the new bluebells, or it could just as well be the other way around, depending on who's doing the listening! OK, sing on everybody, sing O!

What is poetry is for the moving about of biological space with the least amount of lasting damage. It also includes not preventing what has to meet from meeting. Catching casting. Thubble.

—Madeline Gins
from *Good Afternoon, Poetics*

NOTES

Dedication: By "autonauts," I mean slow-time-travelers everywhere including Julio Cortázar and Carol Dunlop who wrote the book on it. (You know who you are.)

Page 6: All meager yawps in this book are really dream-eggs hatched from the Walt Whitman bird, also William Blake and Kenneth Patchen, who sing here too, O!

Page 7: Who decided "Ayekah? Where are you?" (God to Adam post-apple, Genesis 3:9) was a question anyway? הכיא

Page 9: I know physicists must mutter things like "We imagine the world so badly" to themselves all the time, but it wasn't until I read Patchen's line "We imagine one another so badly" in *Poemscape 30*, that I realized how well it fit the bill for everything else.

Page 10: "O isle, unto me" is grifted from Isaiah 49:1's "O isles, unto me; and hearken, ye people, from far; The Lord hath called me from the womb" in order to surf the wave of the whole idea of shrinking distances between peoples, since people are just air anyway, which is also everywhere.

Page 10: The final line of this poem echoes "For I have given you an example, that you should do as I have done to you" John 13:15, on account of its anatomy of death as hope and servitude as life, also being our actual physical anatomy, if you think about it.

Page 15: Peter did not mean the Hudson River when he said "not of perishable seed, but of imperishable, by the word of God, which liveth and abideth forever," 1 Peter 1:23, but if you've ever seen what can survive in the Hudson, then you know he certainly *could* have.

Page 23: This one is from Lewis Carroll, who knew better than anyone that being-in-the-world is so much more expansive than whatever you want to call it, which is just what the duchess tells Alice, "Take care of the sense, and the sounds will take care of themselves." Lewis Carroll, *Alice's Adventures in Wonderland, Chapter 9*

Page 36: But if Bert *doesn't* know you, he'll probably clock you, which is the whole point of *It's a Wonderful Life,* I mean that if the spirit truly be in the body, you can climb onto the people you love and hold onto them until you're finally born.

Page 40: But then there are so many things to unwaveringly believe in, like the sun in your hand that likewise turns your face toward the sun, which also makes you a planet AND a plant, like Hamlet's love for Ophelia, or at least supposedly, but only in a much more literal way on account of star-fire being the *actual* thing that actually moves you, so *really,* never "Doubt thou the stars are fire." Shakespeare, *Hamlet, Act II Scene 2*

Page 45: Just like a butterfly flaps its wings and then there's a tornado in Kansas, so too "Sorrow breaks seasons and reposing hours." Shakespeare, *Richard III, Act I Scene 4,* because really our senses, or *feelings,* don't actually end anywhere, making us both the butterfly and the tornado, and this is very important to remember.

Page 60: Because, honestly, if suffering comes from a tree, who's to say ear stones didn't come from an earthquake? Especially on account of the whole shared wrath element, I mean how "the earth shook and trembled; the foundations also of the hills moved and were shaken, because he was wroth." Psalm 18:7

Page 74: OOOOOOOOOOOOOOOOOOOOOOOOOO "The wind blows where it wishes, and you hear the sound of it." John 3:8

Page 75: Actually not stones but paper! Eighteenth century Jewish philosopher Rabbi Simcha Bunem taught the spiritual practice of carrying two slips of paper in your opposite pockets, one with the words "I am but dust and ashes" (Genesis 18:27) written on it, and then on the other, “For my sake, the world was created.” (Mishnah, Sanhedrin 4:5) But I guess you’d have to ask somebody else to shuffle them for you and put them in your pockets, otherwise wouldn’t you just fish out the latter every time?!

ACKNOWLEDGMENTS

Some of these poems appeared in other forms in *Tagvverk* and *Heavy Feather Review.*

Thank you to my friends and mentors for making life limitless and magical.

Thank you especially to William Waltz and the whole Conduit team for believing in this book.

ABOUT THE AUTHOR

Elizabeth Zuba is the author of the poetry collections *Where Is Everyone!* (Conduit Books & Ephemera), which won the 2024 Minds on Fire Open Book Prize, and *Decoherent The Wing'ed* (SplitLevel Texts); as well as the chapbook *May Double as a Whistle* (The Song Cave). She is also a translator, editor, and art writer.

OTHER TITLES FROM CONDUIT BOOKS & EPHEMERA

Ghost in the Archive by Jennifer Loyd

Bright Life, Animal Heart by Laura Minor

Beneath All Water by Zackary Medlin

Extremely Expensive Mystical Experiences for Astronauts by Dara Barrois/Dixon

Autoblivion by Trey Moody

The Art of Bagging by Joshua Gottlieb-Miller

Thunderbird Inn by Collin Callahan

The Birthday of the Dead by Rachel Abramowitz

The World to Come by David Keplinger

Present Tense Complex by Suphil Lee Park

Sacrificial Metal by Esther Lee

The Miraculous, Sometimes by Meg Shevenock

The Last Note Becomes Its Listener by Jeffrey Morgan

Animul/Flame by Michelle Lewis